920
B
c.1 Blackwood, Alan

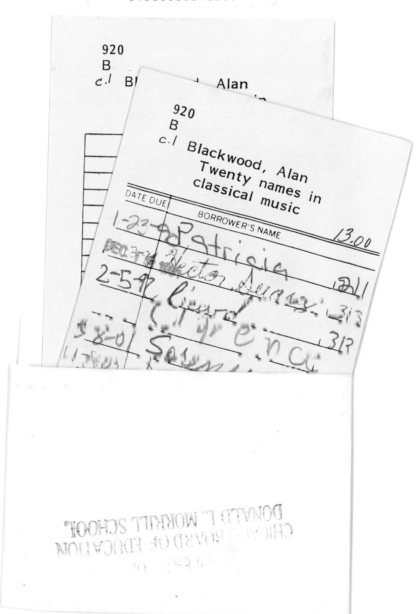

920
B
c.1 Blackwood, Alan
Twenty names in
classical music

DATE DUE	BORROWER'S NAME	
1-23-9?	Patricia	13.00
DEC 3?	Hector Avros	311
2-5-9?	Liard	313
5-8-0?	Clorence	313
	Salomi	

Twenty
Names In
Classical Music

Alan Blackwood

Illustrated by Chris Higham

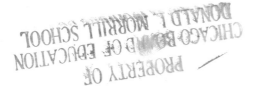
MARSHALL CAVENDISH
New York, London, Toronto

Editor: Rosemary Ashley
Consultant Editor: Maggi McCormick

920
B
c. 1

Reference Edition published 1988

© Marshall Cavendish Limited 1988
© Wayland (Publishers) Limited 1988

Published by Marshall Cavendish Corporation
147 West Merrick Road
Freeport
Long Island
N.Y. 11520

Library of Congress Cataloging in Publication Data

Blackwood, Alan, 1932-
    Twenty names in classical music / Alan Blackwood.
        p. cm. — (Twenty names)
    Bibliography: p.
    Includes index.
    Summary: Presents brief biographies of twenty classical composers.
    ISBN 0-86307-967-9 : $12.95
    1. Composers-Biography-Juvenile literature. [1. Composers.]
I. Title. II. Title: 20 names in classical music. III. Series.
ML3929.B6 1988
[920]-dc19   88-20995
                                    CIP
                                      AC

Printed in Italy by G. Canale & C. S.p.A. - Turin.

Contents

The world of music

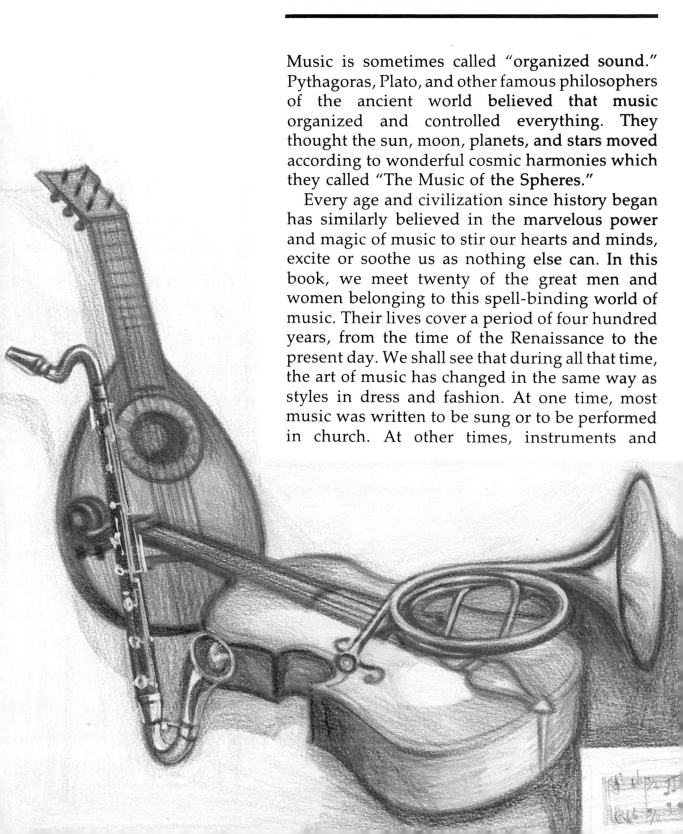

Music is sometimes called "organized sound." Pythagoras, Plato, and other famous philosophers of the ancient world believed that music organized and controlled everything. They thought the sun, moon, planets, and stars moved according to wonderful cosmic harmonies which they called "The Music of the Spheres."

Every age and civilization since history began has similarly believed in the marvelous power and magic of music to stir our hearts and minds, excite or soothe us as nothing else can. In this book, we meet twenty of the great men and women belonging to this spell-binding world of music. Their lives cover a period of four hundred years, from the time of the Renaissance to the present day. We shall see that during all that time, the art of music has changed in the same way as styles in dress and fashion. At one time, most music was written to be sung or to be performed in church. At other times, instruments and orchestras were considered more important; or opera was what mattered most. In this century, jazz has added its own exciting sounds to music.

We shall see also that the people featured here all led very different lives. Some worked in palaces or in churches; others struck out on their own. Some wrote music, such as symphonies, concertos and fugues, to special rules; some tried to express their own thoughts and feelings in their music; others were brilliant pianists, violinists, or singers. Many were rich and famous; others suffered misfortune or lived in poverty. Some lived to a ripe old age; others died tragically young.

What brings them all together within the pages of this book is their place in the endlessly fascinating story of music.

1
Claudio Monteverdi

One of the loveliest cities in the world is Venice, and one of its grandest buildings is the cathedral, or basilica, of St. Mark's. It was here that Claudio Monteverdi composed some of his finest music, nearly four hundred years ago.

Monteverdi lived at the same time as Shakespeare. For many years, he was employed as a musician by an Italian nobleman, the Duke of Mantua. Monteverdi entertained the Duke and his court with madrigals, songs for three or four singers, which were very popular in Renaissance Europe. He also composed operas. The very first operas were simply stage plays in which the players sang or chanted their parts instead of just speaking them. Monteverdi's operas were different. He used an orchestra to accompany the singers, and his music was far more dramatic and tuneful than anything that had previously been

1567 born in Cremona, Italy
1583 enters service of the Duke of Mantua as composer and singer of madrigals
1607 first performance of opera *La Favola d'Orfeo* (The Story of Orpheus)
1613 Leaves court of Mantua and appointed Director of Music in Venice
1642 composes last opera, *L'Incoronazione di Poppea)* (The Coronation of Poppea)
1643 dies in Venice

Right *Renaissance musicians performing madrigals, one of the most popular types of entertainment in Monteverdi's time.*

heard. His works really established opera as an exciting new kind of music.

When the Duke of Mantua died, Monteverdi moved to neighboring Venice, then a very rich and powerful city with its own government. As Director of Music to the Venetian Republic, he composed more operas, and he wrote church music for St. Mark's. The interior of this magnificent building has many galleries and corners, which inspired Monteverdi to divide his choir up, so that the sound of their voices answered each other from different parts of the building. This use of a choir is called "antiphonal," meaning "sounding across." All those years ago, Monteverdi was creating the kind of sound effects we now get from modern stereophonic equipment!

Above *The Doge's Palace in Venice, the city where Monteverdi lived and worked for many years.*

2
Johann Sebastian Bach

No one has ever worked harder than Johann Sebastian Bach. His whole life was spent working for other people, either at one of the princely courts in Germany, or writing and performing music for the Church.

As organist at the chapel of the Duke of Weimar, Bach composed hundreds of pieces for the organ, especially fugues, which are a special way of using a musical theme over and over again. As kapellmeister (court composer) to another German prince, he was paid to write many suites, or sets of dances, for the harpsichord, the cello, or the court orchestra. Finally, he was appointed choirmaster and organist at the big church and school of St. Thomas in Leipzig. There, he had to write a new cantata (setting a religious text to music) for the choir to sing each Sunday through the year – the piece known as "Jesu Joy of Man's Desiring" comes from one of these.

In addition to all this, Bach was a devoted family man. When his first wife died, he soon married again and raised a large family, including several sons, some of whom became famous musicians in their turn.

Bach was much admired in his own lifetime as an organist, but his music was soon forgotten after he died. For nearly a hundred years, it was neglected, until other composers and conductors,

1685	born in Eisenach, Germany
1703	appointed organist at the church at Arnstadt
1707	marries his cousin, Maria Barbara
1708	appointed organist at the court of Saxe-Weimar
1717	appointed Kapellmeister at court of Anhalt-Cöthen, where he composes the "Brandenburg Concertos"
1720	Maria Barbara dies; marries Anna Magdalena Wilcken
1723	appointed Cantor at the church and school of St. Thomas, Leipzig, where he composes the *St. Matthew Passion*
1750	dies in Leipzig

Right *Bach with his wife and children. He was a devoted family man as well as a great composer.*

notably Mendelssohn, began to realize how marvelous it was and to perform it again. Today, the fugues and other pieces for the organ, the "Brandenburg Concertos" for orchestra, and great choral works like the *St. Matthew Passion* and Mass in B minor, are revered as some of the greatest music ever written – from the pen of a man who was a humble servant all his life.

Below *Bach was highly praised as an organist; organ builders often asked his advice when designing a new instrument for a church.*

3
George Frideric Handel

King George II of England was so moved by the sound of the "Hallelujah Chorus" that he rose to his feet and remained standing for the rest of the piece. The occasion was a performance of *Messiah* – a triumph for its composer, George Frideric Handel.

Handel first came to England from Germany in 1710, hoping to make his fortune writing operas. In those days, opera was the most popular and exciting type of entertainment; and the singers, especially the castrati (men who still sang with a boy's voice), were treated like pop stars. For many years, Handel was very successful in London, composing operas with such lovely melodies as the one known as his "Largo."

Below *Handle wrote his "Music for the Royal Fireworks" for a firework display to celebrate a peace treaty in 1748.*

1685 born in Halle, Germany
1705 first opera produced in Hamburg
1706 visits Italy and meets the famous composer, Corelli
1710 settles in London, mainly composing opera music
1717 composes "Water Music" for King George I
1737 suffers a stroke, but recovers his health
1742 first performance of *Messiah* in Dublin
1752 unsuccessful eye surgery leaves him blind
1759 dies in London

Then, English audiences suddenly tired of this spectacular kind of "baroque" opera, and Handel lost all his money. The strain and worry also made him ill. But he was a big, strong man – people called him the "Great Bear" – and not easily beaten. As soon as he was better, he began a new chapter of his career, writing oratorios – similar to operas, but with a religious theme. These, especially *Messiah*, made him even more famous. He also wrote some very popular instrumental pieces, including "Water Music" for a royal boating party on the Thames, and the "Music for the Royal Fireworks," celebrating a peace treaty.

Like Bach back in Germany, Handel finally went blind. He could not compose any more, but he could still play the organ and direct performances of his oratorios (many of them in aid of charities), which he did almost up to the day he died. Handel died in London in 1759, a much-loved figure in England, and was buried in Westminster Abbey.

Above *Handel, at about the time he composed his greatest oratorio,* Messiah.

4
Wolfgang Amadeus Mozart

There have been many child prodigies in music, but none more famous than Wolfgang Amadeus Mozart. He could play the harpsichord at the age of three and was composing little pieces by the time he was five. His father, Leopold, took his "wonderchild" all over Europe, where he played before kings and emperors. Never did anybody have such a fantastic start in life.

Mozart's problems began when he grew up. He lived at a time when almost every artist was employed either by a rich aristocrat or by the Church. Mozart never found the right employer, or patron, who understood his genius. This did not worry him at first. He moved from his home-town of Salzburg in Austria to the capital, Vienna, sure that he could make his own way in the world.

He composed beautiful symphonies, concertos, and string quartets, and such popular pieces as the serenade *Eine Kleine Nachtmusik* (A Little Night Music), in the Classical style of the eighteenth century. He also wrote marvelous operas, including *The Marriage of Figaro* and *Don Giovanni* (based on the life of the legendary lover Don Juan).

His operas were a success; but Mozart was a poor businessman, and he made very little money from them. Then, his wife Constanze became ill, and he had to beg for money from his friends to look after her. Finally, his own health began to fail. He managed to finish another wonderful opera, *The Magic Flute*, and began work on a Requiem Mass. In 1791, he died, at the age of thirty-five, before he could finish the Mass. His funeral was such a miserable affair that afterward nobody could find his grave. But, not long after his death, Mozart was being hailed as one of the greatest geniuses of all time.

Above *An engraving illustrating Mozart's opera* The Magic Flute. *It is an unusual opera, partly serious and partly pantomime.*

Left *Mozart, the child musician, amazed and delighted everyone who heard him.*

13

5
Ludwig van Beethoven

Ludwig van Beethoven lived during the period of the French Revolution and the Napoleonic Wars. He believed in the revolutionary call of "liberty, equality, brotherhood;" and he changed the course of music just as dramatically as Napoleon changed the course of history. He composed symphonies, concertos, string quartets, and sonatas in the Classical style of W. A. Mozart and Joseph Haydn, both of whom had lived and worked in the years just before him. But he filled his works with music of such power and drama that nothing in the whole world of art was ever the same again.

Beethoven himself was a new kind of hero. When he moved to Vienna from his hometown of Bonn in Germany, he soon had rich aristocratic

1770 born in Bonn, Germany
1792 studies with Haydn in Vienna and settles there
1800 composes "Moonlight" Sonata
1802 writes "Heiligenstadt Testament," in which he confesses the start of deafness and hints at suicide
1804 composes Third (*Eroica*) Symphony
1805 first performance of his only opera, *Fidelio*
1806–7 composes Fifth and Sixth (*Pastoral*) symphonies
1809 composes Fifth ("Emperor") Concerto while Napoleon bombards Vienna
1824 first performance of Ninth ("Choral") Symphony
1827 dies in Vienna

Below *Beethoven "heard" music in his head and was able to write it straight down on to paper.*

patrons, who paid him to write music and arranged concerts for him. But the composer would never produce music just to please them; instead, he insisted on his right as an artist to create the music he wanted.

Beethoven also had to fight against growing deafness, the very worst affliction for a musician. In compositions such as his "Moonlight" Sonata, "Eroica" Symphony, and "Emperor"' Piano Concerto, he showed the world that he had triumphed over his handicap.

One of Beethoven's greatest works was his "Choral" Symphony, in which he proclaimed in words, as well as music, his belief in the kindred spirit of humankind. At the end of the first performance, the composer had to be turned around to see the audience clapping and cheering, because he could not hear them. Three years later, he died. Thousands of ordinary men and women joined his funeral procession through the streets of Vienna to pay their last respects to a truly heroic man.

Above *A contemporary portrait of Beethoven at work on a score.*

6
Niccolò Paganini

People said he had made a pact with the Devil, because of the amazing way he could play the violin, and because he looked so strange and sinister – very tall and thin, with long, black hair and eyes sunk deep into his craggy face.

The Italian musician, Niccolò Paganini, was certainly a sensation. He lived at a time when public concerts were just becoming fashionable, and musicians who could play exceptionally well were the new stars of the age. They were called virtuosi, and Paganini was the king of them all. He traveled all over Europe, to Vienna, Paris, Warsaw, London, Edinburgh, thrilling audiences everywhere, playing pieces of his own music which were so difficult that nobody else could play them. He also delighted and astonished audiences with such tricks as performing music on one string only, or even managing to play the violin upside down!

Above *Paganini's strange appearance and amazing skill inspired rumors that he was in alliance with the Devil.*

Paganini was a great showman, but there was a more serious and important side to his career. He developed ways of using the bow to produce a stronger, richer sound, or getting it to bounce rapidly on and off the strings to produce very short, sharp, staccato notes. He also perfected such techniques as playing pizzicato (plucking the strings with the finger). And, in such compositions as his twenty-four caprices, he created a whole new world of sound for the violin.

When he died, Paganini left behind him a collection of violins and violas made by the great Italian instrument-makers Niccolà Amati, Antonio Stradivari, and Giuseppe Guarneri. Stringed instruments made by these and other famous craftsmen are now almost priceless, and they still sound incredibly beautiful, just as they must have when Paganini played them.

1782 born in Genoa, Italy
1795 embarks on first European tour as violin virtuoso
1828–31 greatest years as virtuoso player, with visits to Vienna, Paris, and London
1840 dies in Nice

Below *In the days before radio, records, and tapes, Paganini made a fortune as a traveling virtuoso musician.*

7
Hector Berlioz

His friends called Berlioz "Mad Hector of the flaming locks," because of his thick, reddish hair and his wild and excitable behavior.

He was born in France during the Napoleonic Wars and went to Paris to study medicine. But, he soon gave up medicine and began studying music instead. One day, at a performance of Shakespeare's play, *Hamlet*, he fell madly in love with a member of the cast, a young Irish actress named Harriet Smithson. His feelings about her inspired him to compose his *Fantastic Symphony*, in which he portrayed in music the fantasies and nightmares brought on by his own half-crazy love. Such vivid music, with a grim "March to the Scaffold" and a terrifying "Witches' Dance," had never been heard before.

Berlioz was a pioneer of the Romantic Movement, when composers put more and more of their own feelings and ideas into their music. He wrote for the orchestra in an entirely new way, too, blending the different instruments to create special sound effects, much as an artist mixes colors in a painting. He wrote more vivid and

1803 born near Grenoble, France
1821 studies medicine in Paris, but gives it up in favor of music
1830 composes *Fantastic Symphony*
1841 separates from his wife
1843 tours Germany, Russia, and England, conducting his own music
1863 first performance of part of his opera *The Trojans* in Paris
1869 dies in Paris

brilliant pieces for the orchestra, including his overtures *Roman Carnival* and *Le Corsaire*, a "sound-picture" of a fierce North African pirate. He composed other pieces for big open-air ceremonies, using an orchestra and a chorus of hundreds.

Nearly everything Berlioz composed was new, exciting, larger-than-life. It was too bewildering for most people, and he had a difficult time trying to persuade people to listen to his music. His greatest work was a huge opera, *The Trojans*, about the legendary Trojan Wars, with a tremendous scene involving the famous Wooden Horse of Troy. But the opera was not successful, and its failure broke his heart. He died in 1869, a sad and bitter man.

Above *The Paris Opera House in the 1840s.*

Below *Besides composing many great works, Berlioz was celebrated as a conductor. He was one of the first musicians to conduct orchestras in the way we know today.*

8
Franz Liszt

Franz Liszt was known as "the Paganini of the piano." He lived at a time when the piano was changing from an instrument still not much bigger than a harpsichord to the mighty grand piano we know today. Just as Paganini was the most famous violinist in the world, so Liszt, too, traveling all over Europe, was hailed as the greatest of all piano virtuosi. He was also young and handsome: women often screamed or fainted at his concerts, and he had many love affairs.

There was, however, a much more serious side to Liszt. "I can't perform like a conjurer or a clever dog," he said. He settled in the small, peaceful German town of Weimar, where he composed his exciting Hungarian Rhapsodies, based on the folk music of his homeland; a great sonata and other

Above *As a young man, Liszt was one of the most glamorous personalities of his time – no one played the piano quite like him.*

major piano pieces; and symphonic poems for the orchestra, which described, in music, a story or a scene, and were typical of the Romantic period of art and music in which he lived. He also made arrangements, or transcriptions, for the piano of great orchestral works by other composers (such as Beethoven's symphonies), which were very helpful to music-lovers before the days of radios, record players, and tapes.

In Weimar, Liszt also gave generous help and encouragement to other struggling composers, including Berlioz (page 18) and Wagner (page 22), by arranging performances of their music; and he gave piano lessons to a whole generation of other famous pianists.

Liszt did not remain in Weimar for the rest of his life. He loved Italy and England; and one of his last engagements was to play the piano for Queen Victoria at Windsor Castle. By then, aged seventy-five, he had become a legend in his own lifetime.

Above *There are many caricatures of Liszt. Here, he is shown with eight arms, attacking a piano until it breaks!*

1811	born in Raiding, Hungary
1820	gives his first piano recital
1823–4	visits France and England on concert tours
1848	appointed Kapellmeister at the court of Weimar, Germany
1853–6	composes Hungarian Rhapsodies, *Faust* and *Dante* symphonies
1860	leaves Weimar and settles in Rome
1886	dies in Bayreuth, Germany, while attending Wagner festival

9
Richard Wagner

Richard Wagner wanted to change the world. In 1849, he took part in a political uprising in Germany and was afterward hunted by the police. In exile in Switzerland, he wrote hundreds of books and articles explaining his ideas about politics, philosophy, religion, and art. He also composed such vivid and exciting operas as *The Flying Dutchman*, about a sea captain who sails the ocean in a phantom ship, and *Tannhäuser*, the strange story of a medieval knight. But, Wagner was still not satisfied. He wanted to create an entirely new kind of opera, or "music-drama," which would be music, poetry, philosophy, and religion, all in one. "The Art of the Future," he called it.

Two men, especially, helped to make all Wagner's dreams come true. One was Franz Liszt, who staged the first performance of Wagner's

1813 born in Leipzig, Germany
1840 composes first important opera, *The Flying Dutchman*
1849 takes part in political uprising in Dresden, escapes arrest
1857–9 composes *Tristan and Isolde*
1861–2 composes his comic opera, *The Mastersingers of Nuremberg*
1870 marries Cosima von Bülow
1876 first complete performance of *The Ring of the Nibelungs* at the new festival theater at Bayreuth
1883 dies in Venice, but buried at Bayreuth in Germany

opera *Lohengrin* at Weimar, when everyone else said it was too expensive and difficult to perform – Liszt's daughter, Cosima, later married Wagner. The other was King Ludwig II of Bavaria, who was fascinated by the composer's ideas. He helped Wagner to build a special theater in the small German town of Bayreuth, for performances of his greatest masterpiece, *The Ring of the Nibelungs*. This huge work, in four parts, is based on ancient Nordic myths and legends, about gods and goddesses, giants, dragons, and dwarfs (the Nibelungs); and about a golden ring that carries a terrible curse. The most famous music from the work is "The Ride of the Valkyries" – daughters of the god Wotan, who ride across the sky on winged horses.

Wagner's festival theater at Bayreuth still stands, and, every year, people from all over the world flock to it to hear and see performances of his marvelous operas and music-dramas.

Above *Wagner used to invite his friends to listen to his latest work. He would often sing as well as play the piano.*

Left *The Valkyries, the maiden-warriors who rode across the sky carrying dead heroes to Valhalla, their hall of eternal rest.*

10
Giuseppe Verdi

Italy, as we have read on page 6, was the land where opera began. It has also been the home of some of the finest opera composers – Bellini, Donizetti, Rossini, Puccini. Most famous of all was Giuseppe Verdi. His opera *Rigoletto* is the story of a hunchbacked court jester whose desire for revenge against his enemies leads to his own daughter's tragic death. *Il Trovatore* (The Troubadour) tells a story of drama and passion in the Middle Ages. *Aida* is one of the grandest of all operas, set amid the splendors of ancient Egypt. Verdi filled these operas with strong and stirring tunes that people all over the world were soon singing and whistling, and he became an immensely popular figure.

Below *Verdi loved the plays of Shakespeare. His last opera,* Falstaff, *is inspired by the larger-than-life character who appears in several of the plays.*

Above *Verdi directing a performance of his opera* Aida.

Three more of his operas were inspired by Shakespeare's plays, *Macbeth*, *Othello*, and *Falstaff* (about the rotund, ale-quaffing and wily character in several of the plays). Verdi wrote *Falstaff* when he was over eighty years old – no other composer has gone on working to such a wonderfully ripe old age.

Verdi's long and eventful career also had a political aspect. He lived during an important time in Italy's history called the "Risorgimento" (meaning Resurrection, or New Beginning), when the Italian people were fighting for their independence from foreign domination and the unification of their nation.

Verdi supported the movement and introduced the theme of liberty into some of his operas. When Italy eventually became a united and independent nation in 1861, he was elected as a senator to the first Italian parliament. Verdi was loved by his countrymen, as a patriot, a kind and generous man, and a great artist.

1813	born near Parma, Italy
1832	studies music
1842	composes *Nabucco*, his first big success, after tragic death of his wife and two children
1850–2	composes *Rigoletto* and *Il Trovatore*
1860	elected as a deputy to the first Italian parliament
1871	first performance of *Aida* in Cairo
1893	composes last opera, *Falstaff*
1901	dies in Milan

11

Clara Schumann

Clara Schumann shared her life with two of the greatest German composers. The first was Robert Schumann. Their love affair and marriage, in the face of bitter opposition from Clara's father, is one of the most romantic true stories in the pages of musical history. It inspired Schumann to write some of the world's most beautiful love songs; and for several years, Clara herself was blissfully happy as a loving wife and mother. Then, Schumann became mentally ill and had to be

1819 born in Leipzig, Germany (maiden name, Clara Wieck)
1828 makes her debut as pianist, aged nine
1831 first European concert tour
1840 marries composer Robert Schumann
1856 Robert dies. Visits England; start of lifelong friendship with Brahms
1878 appointed Professor of Piano at Frankfurt Conservatory of Music
1896 dies in Frankfurt, Germany

placed in an asylum. Clara saw him for the last time, just a few hours before he died, and his death nearly broke her heart.

A little while before that tragic event, however, a young and still unknown composer had been introduced to Robert and Clara. His name was Johannes Brahms. Robert predicted a great future for the young man; and, after her husband's death, Clara became Brahms's greatest and most valued friend. He sought her opinion and advice on many musical matters, and she lived to see him acclaimed the greatest composer of symphonies and concertos since Beethoven.

Clara Schumann's association with these two musical giants has helped to keep her name alive. But, it has also taken the spotlight away from her own great gifts. For Clara was a brilliant pianist, and she composed a piano concerto as well as many other pieces. So, as a successful concert pianist and composer in her own right, she also kept the torch burning for women at a time when they had very few rights and very little opportunity to excel in any job or profession.

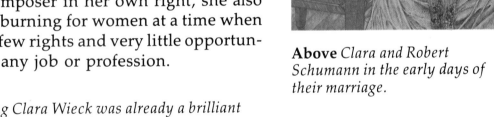

Above *Clara and Robert Schumann in the early days of their marriage.*

Below *The young Clara Wieck was already a brilliant pianist before she married the composer Robert Schumann.*

12
Peter Tchaikovsky

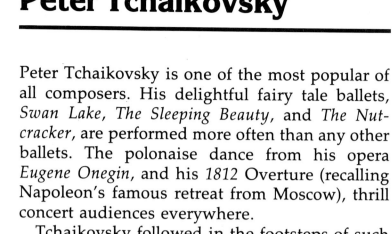

Peter Tchaikovsky is one of the most popular of all composers. His delightful fairy tale ballets, *Swan Lake*, *The Sleeping Beauty*, and *The Nutcracker*, are performed more often than any other ballets. The polonaise dance from his opera *Eugene Onegin*, and his *1812* Overture (recalling Napoleon's famous retreat from Moscow), thrill concert audiences everywhere.

Tchaikovsky followed in the footsteps of such Romantic composers as Berlioz and Liszt, writing vivid, colorful music for the orchestra, which either paints a picture in sound of some scene or event, or is full of personal thought and feeling. In addition to his ballets and operas, he wrote symphonies and concertos, in which he incorporated the exciting sounds of the traditional music of his native Russia.

Surprisingly, however, Tchaikovsky did not lead a dramatic or eventful life, like other

1840	born in Votkinsk, Russia
1863	studies at St. Petersburg (Leningrad) Conservatory of Music
1866	appointed professor at Moscow Conservatory of Music
1875	composes ballet *Swan Lake*
1877	marries but separates from wife almost at once. Begins correspondence with Madame von Meck
1879	first performance in Moscow of opera *Eugene Onegin*
1888	tours Europe and composes ballet *The Sleeping Beauty*
1891	visits US and composes ballet *The Nutcracker*
1893	composes Sixth *(Pathétique)* Symphony; commits suicide in St. Petersburg

Right *A scene from* Swan Lake, *one of the best-loved of all ballets.*

composers such as Berlioz or Liszt. For years on end, at home in Russia, he composed regularly each day, keeping his eye on the clock, just as if he worked in an office. He was a very shy, lonely man. A rich woman named Madame von Meck, who loved his music, sent him money and wrote many letters to him. Although they never actually met, he was very hurt when she suddenly stopped writing to him.

Tchaikovsky began to travel abroad, to Germany, France, England, and the United States, conducting his own music. But he disliked publicity and was always very homesick for Russia.

At the height of his fame, in 1893, Tchaikovsky wrote his *Pathétique* Symphony, meaning a symphony "full of feeling." He said later, "Often while composing it, I shed tears." Not long after finishing the symphony, he took poison and killed himself. It was a tragic end for someone whose work has given so much pleasure to so many millions of people.

Above *St Petersburg in the nineteenth century.*

13
Antonin Dvořák

We call Antonin Dvořák a Czech composer, although when he was alive, there was no such country as Czechoslovakia. His homeland was Bohemia, a region of the old Austrian, or Hapsburg, Empire. But, Dvořák, and his fellow-countryman Bedřich Smetana, hoped that Bohemia would one day be free from Austrian rule and would form part of a new and independent Czech nation.

This hope and desire inspired much of Dvořák's music. The son of a country butcher, he composed pieces such as his Slavonic Rhapsodies and Dances, symphonies and songs filled with the folk melodies of the Bohemian people. Another well-known composition is his "Dumky" Piano Trio (for piano, violin, and cello) based on the Dumka, a traditional type of Slavonic song and dance. With help and encouragement from the great German composer

Right *Dvořák felt a deep sympathy for America's black people when he visited the United States. His* New World Symphony *contains many themes from traditional songs and spirituals.*

Brahms, Dvořák's tuneful, sunny music soon became popular in Europe and the United States, and brought fame both to him and to Bohemia, which was the inspiration for so much of it.

He visited England many times to conduct his own music, and was awarded an honorary music degree by Cambridge University. At the height of his fame, he was also invited to visit the United States. Dvořák was moved by the plight of black people in the United States, who had only recently been freed from slavery. Their work songs and religious spirituals inspired his most celebrated composition, the "New World" Symphony. He also composed his beautiful Cello Concerto in the United States.

There was another, surprising, side to this kindly, lovable man – his great love of railway trains. Dvořák lived in the days of steam locomotives, and he often said that he wished he had invented the steam engine instead of being a composer!

1841	born in Nelahozeves, Bohemia
1857	begins music studies in Prague
1874	wins a national prize for music; gains the help and friendship of Brahms
1878	composes Slavonic Dances and Rhapsodies
1884	makes his first visit to England to conduct his own music
1891	appointed Professor of Composition at Prague Conservatory of Music; visits the US, where he composes his "New World" Symphony
1904	dies in Prague

14
Edward Elgar

Edward Elgar composed most of his music when the British Empire was at the height of its power. His *Cockaigne Overture* is a picture of London, then the largest, richest, and proudest city in the world. His *Pomp and Circumstance Marches* include the noble theme that inspired the words of the patriotic English hymn "Land of Hope and Glory." He became one of the most celebrated and honored men in England.

Elgar's life had been a hard struggle. He was born near Worcester, and there he stayed, a humble church organist and music teacher, until he was forty years old. During that time, he was composing too, but very little of his music was heard. The work that changed all this was his *Enigma Variations* for orchestra. "Enigma" means mystery, and there is a secret behind the beautiful

Above *A photograph of Elgar at about the time he wrote his* Enigma Variations.

theme that begins the piece. But, there is no secret about the variations that follow, which are all musical portraits of the composer's friends. This wonderfully original composition made Elgar famous at last, both in Britain and aboard.

However, fame and fortune did not make him happy for very long. The outbreak of the First World War in 1914, and the horrors of the subsequent fighting, sickened him. By the end of the war, four years later, the British Empire as he knew it was finished. Elgar came to hate "Land of Hope and Glory," and almost stopped composing. He died, in the peace and quiet of the countryside, believing nobody wanted to hear his music any more. But he was wrong. His *Enigma Variations*, his grand and splendid symphonies, and other beautiful, rich-sounding orchestral pieces are loved today as much as they were when they were first performed.

1857	born in Worcester, England
1877	studies the violin in London
1899	first performance of *Enigma Variations*
1900	composes oratorio *The Dream of Gerontius*
1901	composes *Pomp and Circumstance Marches*, which include anthem known as "Land of Hope and Glory"
1904	receives knighthood, the first of many honors
1905	concert tour of US
1934	dies near Worcester

Below *Elgar loved the Cotswolds and the Malvern Hills, the part of England where he was born and where he died.*

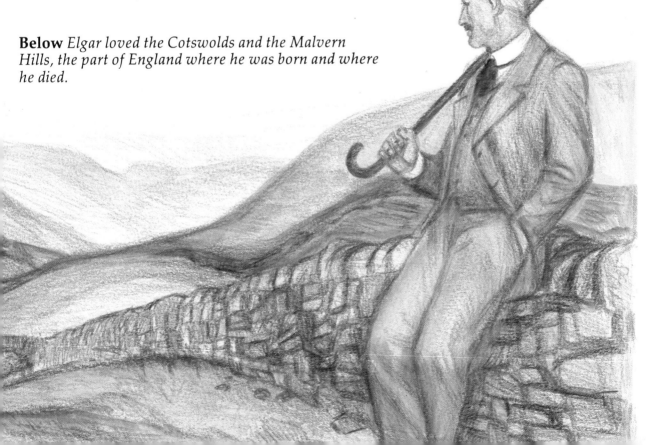

15
Nellie Melba

When Helen Mitchell was born near Melbourne, in 1861, Australia was still a very remote place – a huge empty continent on the far side of the world for most people. Helen (who changed her last name to Melba in honor of the city of Melbourne) made everybody take notice of her homeland.

She was a pianist and organist, but she did not begin to study singing until after her marriage in 1882 to Charles Armstrong. She performed in Sydney and London and then went to Paris to study music. By the time she was thirty years old, she was an international opera star. In those days, she would have been called a "prima donna" – the Italian term for "first lady," or "leading lady" in opera productions. Opera prima donnas were very powerful figures. Melba herself often chose all the other singers she wanted for a production, and even told the producer how she thought an opera should be staged. She was acclaimed in every great opera house in Europe and the United States – Covent Garden, London; the Paris Opera; La Scala, Milan; the Metropolitan Opera, New York – especially for her singing of the part of Mimi, the poor, sick girl in Puccini's opera *La*

1861	born in Richmond, near Melbourne, Australia (real name Helen Mitchell)
1886	completes her musical studies in Paris
1887	makes her London debut
1889	makes her London debut
1893	makes her debuts in Milan and New York
1918	awarded DBE (Dame of the British Empire)
1926	final opera performance in London. Returns to Australia as Director of Melbourne Conservatory of Music
1931	dies in Sydney, Australia

Bohème. Such was her fame that she even had foods named after her. One was Peach Melba, a dish of fresh peaches and ice cream; the other was Melba toast.

Another aspect of Melba's career is now of great historical interest. She was one of the first people to make gramophone recordings. On one occasion, she recorded a duet from *La Bohème* with the equally celebrated Italian singer, Enrico Caruso. This recording is a collector's item among opera lovers today.

Above *Dame Nellie Melba was one of the first musicians to make recordings.*

Below *The prima donna performing one of her great dramatic roles.*

16
Jean Sibelius

Most countries choose political leaders or soldiers as their heroes. For the people of Finland, their greatest hero is a composer, Jean Sibelius.

When he was a young man, he studied law, but he soon decided music was the only thing that mattered to him. One of his early pieces for orchestra was the stirring *Karelia Suite*, named after an old province of Finland (now in the USSR). Then came *Finlandia*, a strongly nationalistic piece of music, which stirred the hearts of all Finnish people at a time when their country was dominated by the old Tsarist Russian Empire. With the performance of *Finlandia*, Sibelius became a national hero. He also became famous in other countries, and he traveled to Italy,

Below *Sibelius as a young man among the lakes and forests of his native land.*

1865	born in Hämeenlinna, Finland
1885	begins music studies at Helsinki Conservatory
1899	composes his best-known work, *Finlandia*
1903	visits England on a concert tour
1914	visits US on a concert tour
1924	composes his Seventh Symphony
1957	dies in Järvenpää, Finland

Germany, England, and the United States to conduct his own compositions. Another piece that soon became popular everywhere was his *Valse Triste* (Sad Waltz).

Sibelius's most acclaimed works are his seven symphonies, sometimes filled with light and beauty, sometimes sounding somber, cold and dark, just like the forests and lakes of his beloved homeland. The symphonies are also highly praised for their very original style.

He composed many other orchestral pieces, inspired by the stories and images of ancient Finnish mythology. One of these is *The Swan of Tuonela*, about a swan that glides to and fro across a river surrounding Tuonela, the remote and mysterious "Land of No Return." Another is *Tapiola* – Tapio is the name of the ancient Finnish god of the forests – and the music includes a marvelous impression of a blizzard sweeping through the dark, lonely forests, with the spirit of Tapio appearing out of the swirling snow.

Above *This monument to Sibelius was erected in Helsinki to commemorate Finland's greatest hero.*

17
Béla Bartók

Below *Bartók spent years among the peasants of Hungary and neighboring Romania, noting down their songs and dances. Their folk music inspired many of his compositions.*

Folk music means "music of the people," music that is a traditional part of the life of a whole race or nation of people, like their clothes and costumes or the kinds of food they eat.

Earlier this century, many composers began to take an interest in folk music. They made sure it would not be forgotten. One of these composers was Béla Bartók in Hungary. The Hungarian people are descended from an ancient Asiatic race called the Magyars. Their land was once part of the old Ottoman Turkish Empire, and their eventful history produced many colorful folk songs and dances.

Bartók traveled all over Hungary and up into the lonely Transylvanian mountains (where Count Dracula was supposed to have lived), asking people in the villages and on the farms to sing or play all the old songs and dances they could remember. He noted these down, or recorded them on an early phonograph. The strange and sometimes wild music he heard inspired his own compositions. But, many people could not understand Bartók's music; and, for a long time, it was neglected.

When Adolf Hitler came to power in Germany and threatened to take over Hungary, Bartók went to live in the United States. But, he was lonely and felt cut off from everything he loved. He was also ill, and he died in New York without ever seeing his beloved homeland again.

By the time of his death, in 1945, people were beginning to realize that Bartók was a great composer, and such compositions as his "Music for Strings, Percussion, and Celesta" and his opera, *Duke Bluebeard's Castle*, were hailed as masterpieces.

1881	born in Nagyszentmiklos, Hungary (now Romania)
1899	studies at Budapest Royal Academy of Music
1905	begins special study of Hungarian and Romanian folk music
1907	appointed Professor of Piano at Budapest Music Academy
1940	emigrates to the US, and composes Concerto for Orchestra
1945	dies in New York City

Igor Stravinsky

At the first performance of *The Rite of Spring* in Paris in 1913, people in the audience started shouting and fighting, and the police were called.

The composer whose music caused all the fuss was Igor Stravinsky. He was born in Russia, when it was still ruled by the Tsars. It was another Russian, Sergei Diaghilev, who made Stravinsky famous. Diaghilev's ballet company, Ballets Russes, was touring France; and, in 1910, he asked Stravinsky to write the music to a new ballet, based on old Russian fairy tales, called *The Firebird*. Stravinsky's music was so brilliant that Diaghilev immediately asked him to write the scores for two more ballets. One of these was *Petrushka*, about three puppets that come to life. The other was *The Rite of Spring*, depicting pagan rituals in ancient Russia. It was the strange, some-

1882 born in Oranienbaum, near St. Petersburg (Leningrad), Russia
1903 studies music with Rimsky-Korsakov in St. Petersburg
1913 first performance in Paris of ballet *The Rite of Spring*
1920 settles in France, composes oratorio *Oedipus Rex* and Symphony of Psalms for Boston Symphony Orchestra
1939 moves to US, composes Symphony in Three Movements
1962 returns to USSR for triumphant concert tour
1971 dies in New York, but buried in Venice

times violent, sound of Stravinsky's music for this last ballet that at first shocked audiences.

Stravinsky never composed anything else like it. During the First World War (1914–18), when most theaters and concert halls in Europe were closed, he lived in Switzerland, writing music for a small traveling theater. Then, he lived for several years in France before settling in the United States. His musical style, like his address, kept changing, so that people wondered what sort of music he would compose next. He remained famous, and was frequently asked by rich patrons and great orchestras to compose pieces especially for them.

In 1962, when he was eighty years old, Stravinsky went back to Russia (by then the USSR) for the first time in more than fifty years. It was a great triumph at the end of a wonderful career, but no other event in his life could quite compare with that first amazing performance of *The Rite of Spring*, back in 1913.

Below *Petrushka, or "Little Pete," the Blackamoor, and the Doll, as they first appeared in Stravinsky's famous ballet.*

George Gershwin

The New York audience stood up and cheered the young composer on the platform. The year was 1924, and George Gershwin had just played for the first time his *Rhapsody in Blue*, for piano and orchestra. It was written in the style of a concerto, but it was full of the rhythms and harmonies of jazz, and it was the first piece of concert music that sounded truly American.

Gershwin's parents were Russian Jews, named Gershovitz, who had emigrated to the United States. George himself was born in Brooklyn and grew up with very little musical training. He began his career playing piano arrangements of other people's songs in Tin Pan Alley, the nickname for New York City's old music publishing district. Soon, he was writing songs of his

1898 born in Brooklyn, New York
1913 works as pianist for New York music publisher
1920 writes his first "hit" song, *Swanee*, made famous by singer Al Jolson
1924 first performance of *Rhapsody in Blue*
1935 first performance of opera *Porgy and Bess*
1937 dies in Hollywood, California

Below *A scene from* Porgy and Bess, *Gershwin's celebrated opera about black people in the American South.*

own, often with words written by his talented brother, Ira. Before long, Geshwin was one of the most successful songwriters on Broadway. His songs and stage shows were hits in London and Paris, too, and he became rich and famous.

But, for George Gershwin, fame and fortune were not enough. He wanted to be a serious composer. He studied with other famous musicians in the United States and Europe. After writing *Rhapsody in Blue*, he composed his Concerto in F, and a colorful orchestral piece titled *An American in Paris*, both containing the same exciting blend of jazz and concert music. Then came his masterpiece, *Porgy and Bess*, an opera about black people in the Deep South, which contained some of Gershwin's loveliest melodies.

When he was only thirty-nine, Gershwin collapsed and died. The whole world was shocked by his sudden death. Thankfully, we have all his wonderful songs, and pieces like *Rhapsody in Blue*, to remind us of his short, but brilliant, life.

Above *George Gershwin (left) and his brother Ira, who wrote many of the lyrics for his songs.*

20
Leonard Bernstein

West Side Story is one of the most exciting and colorful of all stage and screen musicals. It is based on Shakespeare's play *Romeo and Juliet*, but the action takes place in New York City, with battles between two rival street gangs called the Jets and the Sharks. The man who wrote the music for *West Side Story* is the American composer Leonard Bernstein. Another of his very successful musical shows is *On The Town*, about three sailors on a day's shore leave, also set in New York.

In these brilliant musical shows, Bernstein makes clever use of the rhythms and harmonies of jazz and Latin American music, as George Gershwin and other American composers have done. But, he is also a serious composer, interested in music and religion. His *Jeremiah* Symphony is inspired by his Jewish childhood

1918 born in Lawrence, Massachusetts
1935 begins studies at Harvard University
1941 studies at Curtis Institute of Music, Philadelphia
1943 makes his debut as conductor in New York
1944 wins New York Critics' award for his *Jeremiah* Symphony
1957 first performance in New York of *West Side Story*
1969 appointed life conductor of New York Philharmonic Orchestra
1971 composes Mass for opening of John F. Kennedy Arts Center, Washington, D.C.

Below *Leonard Bernstein is one of today's most popular conductors, as well as a composer.*

and includes a setting of words from the Book of Jeremiah in the Bible. Another of his compositions is a most unusual setting of the Christian service of the Mass, which he wrote for the opening of a new concert hall in Washington, D.C., named after President Kennedy.

Bernstein is equally famous as a conductor, regularly appearing with orchestras throughout the world, and making recordings with them. He especially loves to conduct music for a very large orchestra and enjoys works of intensity and drama, such as the symphonies of the Austrian composer, Gustav Mahler. He is also a brilliant concert pianist. Bernstein has written successful books about music and is an experienced broadcaster, often appearing on radio and television to discuss music, as well as to conduct or play the piano. He is one of the most gifted, versatile, and busiest musicians in the world today.

Above *A scene from the stage and screen musical* West Side Story, *set amid the streets and tenements of New York.*

Glossary

Ballet Stage entertainment with music and dancing. Ballet, as we know it, began in France, about 1650.

Baroque music Music written between about 1650 and 1750, including types of opera, oratorio, concertos, and sonatas.

Classical music Strictly speaking, music belonging to the period from 1750 to about 1800, written mainly as symphonies, concertos, string quartets, and sonatas. Also denotes serious art music in general.

Concerto Italian word meaning "playing together;" usually a composition for one solo player and orchestra, in three separate sections, or movements.

Debut First public appearance of a performer.

Fugue Type of musical composition in which a theme is played many times over, so that the notes fit together in a special way. It is known as "contrapuntal" (note against note) music.

Jazz Music with special rhythms and harmonies, first played by black Americans about 1900, but soon spreading all over the world, leading to swing, jive, boogie, rock and pop.

Mass Principal service of the Roman Catholic Church, the words of which have been set to music by many composers.

Opera Italian word meaning "works;" a stage drama with singers and orchestra. The first operas date from around 1600.

Oratorio Composition for choir, soloists and orchestra, much like some kinds of opera, but usually setting religious words to music.

Overture French word meaning "opening;" usually a piece played by the orchestra at the start of an opera, though some overtures have been written as pieces on their own.

Passion Composition for choir, soloists, and orchestra, setting to music the gospel accounts of Christ's trial and crucifixion.

Patron Someone who sponsors and helps musicians.

Romantic music Period of music composed between about 1830 and 1900, often inspired by a story, poem, or painting, or by the composer's personal thoughts and feelings, following the Romantic movement in art and literature.

Sonata Italian word meaning "sounding piece;" usually a composition for piano, or for piano and one other instrument, in three separate sections, or movements.

Staccato Italian word meaning "detached," describing a way of playing notes in a short, sharp manner.

Symphony Greek word meaning "harmonious sounds;" usually a composition for full orchestra in four separate sections, or movements.

Further reading

America, I Hear You: A Story about George Gershwin by Barbara Mitchell (Carolrhoda Books, 1978)

Enjoying the Arts: Music by David Rattner (Rosen, 1976)

European Classical Music by Richard Carlin (Facts on File, 1987)

Music and Sound by Mark Pettigrew (Watts, Franklin, 1987)

Music by Carol Greene (Childrens Press, 1983)

Operantics with Wolfgang Amadeus Mozart by Mary Neidorf (Sunstone Press, 1987)

Pictorial History of Music by Paul H. Lang (W. W. Norton, 1960)

The Story of Music by Mundy (EDC Publishing, 1980)

Your Book of Music by Michael Short (Faber and Faber, 1983)

Index

Picture acknowledgements

Aquarius Picture Library 47; Mary Evans Picture Library 7, 8, 11, 13, 15, 16, 18, 21, 23, 24, 27, 29, 32, 35; Topham Picture Library 45; Zefa 37.